Awakening

A Beginner's Guide

to

Spirituality

Workbook

Facebook *Lighten Up Spirituality*
Email: *LightenUp02@yahoo.com*
Website:
www.lightenupspirituality.com
First Edition, 2025
ISBN: 979-8-9992596-1-5
Cover Art and Design by: Kiana Coulton & Denise Jensen
Printed in the United States of America

May this sacred work reach those it is meant to awaken. May it serve as a lantern of light, a circle of healing, and a guide home to the soul.

Divine Creator, Light of All That Is,

I offer this sacred workbook, born of spirit, as a vessel of awakening, truth, and healing. I infuse each page with Your presence.

Let every word become a lantern, every prompt a mirror, every ritual a bridge between soul and Source.

Guide it now into the hands of every heart that yearns, every soul that seeks, every spirit ready to rise.

May it find the lost, uplift the weary, and rekindle the divine spark in those who have forgotten their light.

May angels walk with this work.

May it be protected, supported, and lovingly received.
Ase – Ase. So it is, and so it shall be.

DEDICATION

FOR THE SEEKER, THE DREAMER, THE REMEMBERER

To all those beautiful spirits experiencing personal moments of awareness and to those who   feel the call in their soul to awaken, to heal, and to come home to the light within-

This sacred guidebook is dedicated to *you*.

May these pages open your heart, stir your memory, and light the lantern of your divine path.

And to the ones *who came before us, walk beside us now, and guide us from the unseen realms-your* love echoes through every word.

Denise

Spirit Sister of Lighten Up Spirituality

Thanks & Dedication

To my wonderful "Mister" Richard Jensen for his continual Love & Support. He has never wavered in his support and encouragement for my path to spiritual growth & enlightenment on my personal mission and journey to aide and guide individuals on their path to finding their personal journey to enlightenment. Creating a positive group of like-minded & supportive souls coming together to form a loving joyous community of spiritually aware individuals to assist the newly "Awakened" who are entering into their AHA phase of spirituality.

None of the wonderful blessings that I have been able to share and give to others would have been possible without his support. His love, kindness, joy for life is so genuine and his laughter has always been so contagious. His belief in me has allowed me to "Shine" my inner light so bright that it also shines on the outside.

I Love you always

Mrs. "J"

Table of Contents

Table of Contents Cont.

INTRODUCTION
Welcome Letter from Spirit

Welcome, to the newly awakened spirit within you. You may have recently had your **AHA** moment.

Realizing that there is something more, something greater than ourselves and it's stirring within you. This energy is your spirit alive and nudging you to get curious to the awareness for higher enlightenment.

However, you are just not sure which direction you are supposed to travel on your personal journey towards your path to enlightenment. If you find yourself thumbing through any of these workbooks looking for guidance and/or direction. Spiritually, that means that your higher guide has brought you to this point to aid you in your starting point.

You hold in your hands not just a book, but a sacred key to your inner world. This workbook is your companion, your mirror, and your guide as you journey deeper into the light of your soul. May these pages be filled with grace, revelation, and courage. Remember: you are not alone.

You walk this path held in love, watched over by Spirit, and uplifted by the positive loving community of Lighten Up.

Intention of this Workbook

This sacred workbook is crafted with love and joy to support your spiritual awakening. Whether you are just beginning your awakening or seeking deeper roots, it offers rituals, teachings, prompts, and soul reflections to nourish every level of your being—heart, mind, body, and soul.

How to Use This Sacred Companion

- Treat it as a living altar—come to it in stillness, reverence, and authenticity.

- Use colored pens, drawings, and pressed leaves or symbols that feel sacred to you.

- There is no right pace. Flow with the moon, the seasons, your energy.

- Revisit chapters at different times of your life they will reveal new truths as you grow.

A Ritual to Bless the Workbook

Gather a white candle, a sprig of rosemary or lavender, and a small bowl of water.

Light the candle and place your hands over the workbook.

Speak aloud:

"With love, I open this sacred space. May every word, page, and reflection in this book awaken the light within me. I dedicate this journey to my highest self and to the healing of all beings.
So it is."

Dip your fingers in the water and anoint the corners of the book. Then hold it to your heart and breathe in its presence. The workbook is now blessed.

SACRED PRAYERS

Prayer of Invocation

I entreat thee to graciously bestow upon me thy heavenly blessing.

Purify my thoughts and actions so that they may be guided by thy divine wisdom, knowing that all things are possible in thy name.

I beseech thee in all humility to fill my whole being with love, compassion, and understanding for all those who come my way.

Bless me with true knowledge and the ability to receive thy everlasting love into my soul, so that I may sincerely seek out the truth in thy holy name.

Help me to rise above my own earthly concerns so I can guide and inspire all those who are in need of love and guidance at this time.

Blessed be

Prayer of Protection

Divine guide within me, I encircle myself in your white light of love and divine protection, keeping me safe from harm— mentally, emotionally, physically, spiritually, and financially.

I ask that any negativity directed toward me or at me bounce off and return to the original bearer. If there is any negativity dwelling within me or around me, I demand that you leave me now and not return this day, so I can be the best me I know how to be—someone full of unconditional love and joy, who's helpful, kind, understanding and supportive to anyone you send my way.

Grant me the wisdom, knowledge, and insight to assist them in the best way I know how. I feel the warmth of your golden light sending comfort and ease to my being, and I feel blessed. My heart is full, and I am grateful.

Love & Light

 **Prayer of Gratitude**

Dear God, Goddess, All That Is,
I come to you this day with a heart full of
unconditional love and gratitude for all the
blessings in my life—blessings you have bestowed
upon me, the many loving people who have
entered my life, sharing with me their joy and
their journey.

I give thanks for the infinite abundance in all
areas of my life—my health, my forever open
heart, my clarity of mind, and my spirit guide to
lead me. I have riches beyond words.

Thank you for my life itself, so I may continue to
be of service, guiding and inspiring others as
they awaken to the spiritual path and embark on
their personal journey. I am grateful for all those
who come my way, sharing and exchanging love
and wisdom.

Thank You for my family and friends, and for the
beauty that surrounds me—the beauty of nature,
all its wonders, and the critters that dwell within
it. The warmth of my home is filled with your
love and light, ready for me to invite and share
with others.

Thank you for the strength, wisdom, and
enlightenment you provide. I am grateful for the
daily bounties of plenty that you gift to me
***EVERYDAY**. Help me never to take these*
blessings for granted and always find ways to
share your love and kindness with others.

CHAPTER ONE: AWAKENING

"To awaken is to remember the divine spark within."

What Is Spiritual Awakening?

Spiritual awakening is the soul's gentle—or sometimes jarring—remembrance that there is more to life   than what meets the eye. It is a stirring within—often triggered by a life event, loss, break through, or an inner longing—that calls you to seek deeper truths, expanded awareness, and alignment with your higher self. Awakening is not a destination but a sacred unfolding. It is the process of peeling away illusions to uncover your divine essence.

At its heart, spiritual awakening is the moment you begin to **see with the soul.** The physical world no longer feels like the full story. You begin to sense energy, synchronicity, guidance, and connection beyond the five senses. Old patterns may fall away, values may shift, and your heart opens to something vaster, more loving, and more eternal.

This awakening often comes in waves—sometimes as subtle whispers, sometimes as storms of transformation. You may question who you are, what you believe, or what your true purpose is.

These questions are not signs of losing your way, but signs that your spirit is beginning to remember.

Awakening is also deeply personal. For some, it may come through meditation or nature. For others, through heartbreak, illness, or spiritual study. No two paths are the same, yet all are sacred. It is a return to truth, to love, to light. A reclaiming of your place in the greater mystery of the Universe.

Opening Meditation: Awakening

"Breath of Awakening"

Close your eyes and place your hands gently over your heart. Take a deep breath in, and as you exhale, allow your body to soften. Breathe again and feel the stirring within—a whisper of your soul calling you home.

Invite your Spirit Guides and Highest Self to walk beside you now.

Silently speak:
"I am ready to awaken. I open my heart to the truth of who I am. Let this chapter ignite the light within me."

Rest for a few breaths, and when you are ready, begin.

As you awaken, you may:

- Feel more connected to intuition and inner guidance.
- Become aware of synchronicities and divine timing.
- Seek authenticity, compassion, and soulful living.
- Release limiting beliefs, wounds, or fear-based patterns.
- Sense a call to serve, heal, or inspire others.
- Experience moments of stillness, awe, or deep inner peace.

The journey is not always easy, but it is always holy. And the beautiful paradox is this: you are not becoming someone new— you are remembering who you truly are.

Journal Prompt
"When did I first feel the call to awaken?"

Write about a moment in your life when you felt something shift. What stirred within you? What did you begin to question? How did it change the way you viewed the world?

Your Personal Awakening Timeline

Create a visual or written timeline of your spiritual journey so far. Include:

- Moments of joy and loss
- Spiritual teachers or guides
- Books, dreams, or signs that inspired change
- Turning points where you knew you were awakening

Reflection: What Is My Soul Seeking?

Spend time in meditation or stillness. Then, journal your soul's desires using this prompt:

"At this stage of my path, my soul is calling me to..."

Ritual: Candle Meditation for Clarity

Materials: A white or violet candle, a quiet space, and a notebook. Light the candle and gaze gently into the flame. Let your breath deepen, in through the nose, taking in fresh energy, take a 3 second hold at its peak then slowly let out through pursed lips releasing all negative energy. Imagine the flame burning away illusions and bringing the truth of your soul to light. When ready, write down any messages, symbols, or insights that arise.

Affirmation:

"I am awake, aware, and aligned with the light of my soul."

Awakening Reflections

Awakening Reflections

Reflections

CHAPTER TWO:

THE ART OF MEDITATION

"Go where you are needed. Find those who are ready. Be a guide, a light, a friend."

What Is Meditation?

Meditation is the ancient art of turning inward—a sacred pause from the noise of the outer world to connect with your inner stillness. It is not about emptying the mind or achieving perfection, but about becoming present to what is. Through meditation, we learn to observe our thoughts rather than become entangled in them, creating space for clarity, peace, and insight to rise.

Across traditions and cultures, meditation has long been a pathway to spiritual awakening, emotional healing, and deepened awareness. It is a practice of remembrance—of returning to your breath, your body, your being—and awakening to the divine presence within. In this space of stillness, your soul whispers and your heart soften, and even a few moments of intentional breath can reconnect you to something greater.

The Purpose of Meditation

- Strengthens connection to your higher self and inner wisdom.
- Reduces stress and anxiety.
- Opens the heart to compassion and clarity.
- Supports emotional healing and spiritual awakening.
- Builds mindfulness, patience, and presence.

How to Meditate

Basic Steps:

- Find a quiet space.
- Sit or lie down comfortably.
- Close your eyes and bring attention to your breath.
- When thoughts arise, gently return to your breath. Refocus on: Taking a deep breath in and slowly releasing.
- Start with 3–5 minutes, gradually increasing as it feels natural.

Take a deep meditation breathe in through the nose and slowly release **ALL** air through perched lips.

This represents meditations basic principle "In with the positive and out with the negative". Do this process 3 times, then breathe normally.

Helpful Tips:

- Use a timer with a soft chime.
- You can place one hand on your heart and one on your belly.
- Keep a meditation journal to note insights or feelings afterward.

Opening Meditation: The Art of Meditation

"Return to Stillness"

- Sit quietly and bring your awareness to the breath.
- Inhale slowly through your nose, and exhale softly through your mouth.
- Feel the stillness growing within you like a sacred lake.

Say silently or aloud:
"I return to the stillness that has always lived within me. I open myself to peace, presence, and the whispers of my soul."

Invite your guides to hold space for you in silence. Remain here for a few moments, then gently begin   your journey into the chapter.

Types of Meditation to Explore

- Breath Awareness – Focus solely on breathing.
- Guided Visualization – Listen to imagery- based guidance.
- Mantra Meditation – Repeating a sacred word or phrase.
- Loving-Kindness (Metta) – Sending love   to self and others.
- Walking Meditation – Mindful movement outdoors or indoors.

Common Challenges
&
How to Work Through Them

- *"I can't stop thinking."* That's normal—just notice and come back.
- *"I fall asleep."* Try meditating upright or earlier in the day.
- *"I don't have time."* Even one mindful breath is meditation.

Sacred Ritual:

Creating a Meditation Practice

Mini Ritual:

- Light a candle or incense

- Place a comforting item nearby (crystal, journal, photo, etc.)

- Begin with a simple intention: *"I give myself this moment to simply be."*

- Sit, breathe, and receive

Affirmations for Meditation

- *"I am present in this moment."*
- *"My mind is calm; my heart is open."*
- *"I return to my breath, again and again."*
- *"In stillness, I hear my soul."*

Meditation Inspirations

Spiritual Insights

_____

_____

_____

_____

_____

_____

_____

_____

_____

_____

_____

_____

_____

_____

_____

_____

Reflections

CHAPTER THREE: CREATING SACRED SPACE

"Where you dwell becomes a temple when you live with awareness."

—*Unknown*

What Is a Sacred Space?

A sacred space is more than a physical place— it is a vibration, an intention, a sanctuary where the spirit is free to breathe.

It can be a corner of your home, a quiet garden path, a sunlit room, or even a space you carry within. What makes it sacred is not *what* fills it, but *how* you fill it—with presence, reverence, and love.

In a sacred space:

- You are invited to **pause** the outside world.
- You are encouraged to **listen** inward.
- You are safe to be **authentically yourself**—no masks, no demands, no performance.

A sacred space honors your soul's longing to connect—with the Divine, with your guides, with your inner truth.

It becomes a mirror for your spirit and a bridge to your higher self. You might adorn it with candles, crystals, feathers, incense, sacred texts, or simply silence. But no object is required—the power comes from your **intention**. When you declare a space sacred, you are declaring yourself sacred within it.

Let it be:

- A place to pray, meditate, journal, or cry.
- A place to remember who you truly are.
- A place to rest in the arms of the universe.

You are worthy of sacred space. You are worthy of stillness and beauty. And as you create space for spirit—you will find that spirit fills you in return.

Opening Meditation: Creating Sacred Space

"Sanctuary Within"

Close your eyes and place one hand over your heart, the other resting gently on your belly. Breathe in deeply... and slowly exhale.

With each breath, imagine clearing space within you—sweeping away noise, clutter, and distraction. Feel your breath preparing the temple of your spirit.

Call upon your spiritual guides, guardians, and the wisdom of the Earth to surround you now.

Silently or aloud, speak this intention:
"I enter this chapter as sacred space. I am safe, I am guided, I am open to the energies that support my healing and transformation."

Rest for a few moments, allowing your inner sanctuary to unfold... and when you are ready, begin.

How to Build an Altar

An altar is a spiritual focal point where the divine and the human meet. Your altar can include:
- A cloth, table runner, scarf etc. to set the tone (color matters!).
- A white candle to symbolize light and Spirit.
- Crystals or stones for grounding, intention, spiritual awareness, love and clarity.
- Images of deities, ancestors, angels, or spirit animals.
- Natural items like feathers, shells, or leaves.
- A small bowl for offerings (herbs, coins, or flowers).

Place your altar somewhere you will see it often. Let it evolve with the seasons, moon cycles, or your emotional state and spiritual growth.

Crystals, Scents, Colors & Symbols

- **Crystals:**
  Amethyst (peace), *Rose Quartz* (love), *Citrine* (abundance), *Black Tourmaline* (protection), *Clear Quartz* (amplification and clarity)

- **Scents:**
  Lavender (calm), *Sage* (cleansing),

- *Frankincense* (divine connection), *Sweetgrass* (invitation*)*

- **Colors:**
  White (purity and clarity), *Purple* (spiritual wisdom), *Pink* (unconditional love), *Green* (healing and heart energy), *Blue* (truth and expression), *Yellow* (joy and confidence), *Black* (protection and grounding)

- **Symbols:**
  Use what speaks to you—animal totems, chakra

Ritual: Blessing Your Space

Gather your items, light a candle, and walk clockwise around your space.

Say aloud:

*"I cleanse this space with love and light.
May only peace and divine presence dwell here. This is a sanctuary for healing, clarity, and sacred connection."*

Sprinkle salt or flower petals, or use sound (a bell or chime) in each corner. Stand in the center and breathe deeply.

Journal Prompt

"What elements make me feel spiritually safe and supported?"

List or draw your ideal sacred space. What textures, colors, sounds, and scents call you home to yourself?

Affirmation

"I am held in sacred space, within and around me."

Meditation
Inspirations

_____

_____

_____

_____

_____

_____

_____

_____

_____

_____

_____

 # Spiritual Insight

_____

_____

_____

_____

_____

_____

_____

_____

_____

_____

_____

_____

_____

<u>Reflections</u>

_____

_____

_____

_____

_____

_____

_____

_____

_____

_____

CHAPTER FOUR:

INTENTION & MANIFESTATION

"Your thoughts are seeds. Your feelings are sunlight. Your faith is the water that makes them grow."

Setting Intentions &Manifestation

"Energy flows where intention goes." — *Hawaiian Proverb*

Creating sacred space is more than physical design—it is an act of energetic alignment. Once your space is cleared and blessed, you open the portal to co-creation. This is where intention and manifestation come in.

Opening Meditation: Aligning With Your Sacred Intention

"I Become What I Intend"

This meditation is best done in a quiet space, with a candle lit and one hand over the heart.

Close your eyes.
Take a deep breath in through your nose...
and out through your mouth.

Again, slower this time...
Feel your body begin to soften.
Feel your mind begin to clear.
Feel your soul begin to listen.

The Visualization

Imagine you are standing in a vast open space— safe, quiet, and filled with soft golden light. Before you is a pool of still water, like a mirror.
You step closer and gaze into it.

Now, see your highest self-reflected back to you—radiant, peaceful, fulfilled.
This is the version of you who has already embodied your sacred intention.
They are not waiting, chasing, or striving.
They are living the very energy you long to become.

Ask this version of yourself silently:

- "What do you know that I have forgotten?"

- "What do I need to release to meet you?

- "What is one step I can take today to align with you?"

Listen. Trust what comes.

Anchor the Intention

Now place your hand on your heart and whisper your sacred intention aloud or within:

"I am ready to align with my truth."
"I receive what is in harmony with my soul."
"I become what I intend."

See your intention become a glowing light in your heart. Watch it pulses. Watch it grow. This is your co-creation seed—planted in sacred ground.

Closing

Take another deep breath.

Wiggle your fingers and toes gently.

And when you're ready, open your eyes.

You are aligned. You are empowered. You are the magic.

What is an Intention?

An Intention is **the soul's whisper made visible.** It is the sacred act of choosing your energy on purpose. When you set an intention, you are declaring to the Universe:

"This is the energy I choose to embody. This is the direction I wish to grow."

Unlike goals, which are focused on achievement, **intentions are rooted in presence.**

They are not about what you do, but *how you do it*— with mindfulness, love, and alignment. An intention might sound like:

- *"I choose to move through this day with grace."*
- *"I open myself to healing."*
- *"I welcome joy into my heart."*

Intention gives your thoughts structure, your rituals power, and your journey purpose.

It becomes the thread that connects your actions to your spiritual path. It's not just what you want—it's **who you're willing to become** in order to receive it.

Affirmation:
"My intentions are clear. My heart is open. I trust the unfolding."

What is Manifestation?

Manifestation is the sacred unfolding of your inner world into outer form.
It is a co-creative process between your energy, your intention, and the Universe.
We are always manifesting—through our thoughts, beliefs, emotions, and actions.
But conscious manifestation is when we align our soul with Spirit and deliberately create what is in our highest good.
True manifestation is not about force or control. It is about vibrational alignment, spiritual trust, and the inner belief that you are worthy of receiving.

Manifestation requires:
- Clarity of desire.
- Emotional alignment with which you desire.
- Letting go of resistance and fear.
- Patience and trust in divine timing.

It is both magical and practical. Energetic and embodied. When your intention and vibration match your desire, the Universe responds—in seen and unseen ways.

Sacred Reminder:
"You do not chase what is meant for you. You align with it—and it arrives."

How Manifestation Works Spiritually

Manifestation is the natural outcome of aligned thought, emotion, and action. It is not about "getting" but about becoming—shifting your energy into resonance with what you desire. Your sacred space acts as a physical reminder of your spiritual blueprint.

How to Set a Sacred Intention

1. Center Yourself – Sit quietly. Breathe into your heart space.

2. Clarity is Key – Focus on one area of your life: love, health, creativity, purpose.

3. Write It in the Now – Phrase it as already true.

"I am open to receiving loving and nourishing relationships."

"I create from joy and am supported in my purpose."

Place It on Your Altar – Fold it and place it under a crystal or in a sacred vessel.

Repeat it daily. Feel it. Speak it aloud. Anchor it in your being.

Manifestation Ritual: Candle & Crystal Grid

Tools: A candle, 3–5 small crystals, paper, and a symbol (like a feather or key)

1. Create a Grid – Place crystals in a circle or triangle around your intention paper.

2. Light the Candle – Visualize your intention illuminated in light.

3. Speak the Intention – Let your voice declare   it with emotion.

4. Close with Trust – Say:

"I surrender this to Divine timing. I am aligned and open to receive."

Let the candle burn for a few minutes each day, returning to this sacred act with devotion.

Journal Prompt

"What am I ready to call in, claim, or create at this   time in my life?"

Affirmation

"I am a conscious creator. My intentions are blessed, clear, and aligned with divine love."

 # Intentions

_____

_____

_____

_____

_____

_____

_____

_____

_____

_____

_____

 _____

Manifestation Note

_____

_____

_____

_____

_____

_____

_____

_____

_____

_____

_____

 _____

Reflections

_____

_____

_____

_____

_____

_____

_____

_____

_____

_____

CHAPTER FIVE:

ENERGY AND THE AURA

"You are not just a body. You are a radiant field of living light."

Opening Meditation:
Energy, the Aura & Smudging

"Cleansing Light"

Sit quietly and imagine a soft golden light surrounding your body. Breathe in deeply and exhale slowly.
With each breath, feel this light clearing your energy field—washing away tension, heaviness, or worry.

Visualize the aura around you glowing brighter with every breath, like a protective halo of love and clarity.

Silently speak this intention:
"I cleanse my energy with light and love. I open to the wisdom of my aura and welcome the power of sacred clearing."

Call in your guides to assist in releasing what no longer serves.

Breathe... and when you feel clear, begin the chapter with an open and vibrant spirit.

The Nature of Energy

All life is energy. Every thought, word, action, and emotion send out a frequency. You are both a transmitter and a receiver — constantly exchanging vibrations with the universe around you. The quality of your energy affects your health, relationships, manifestations, and spiritual clarity.

Energy cannot be destroyed, only transformed. When you begin to understand this, you awaken to your personal power. You begin to realize:

"I am not just in the world. The world is in me. My energy shapes my reality."

When you raise your vibration — through love, compassion, gratitude, and conscious living — you become a light in the darkness, a healing presence, and a vessel for divine grace.

Understanding Your Aura

The **aura** is your spiritual atmosphere — a luminous, multi-layered energy field that surrounds your physical body. It reflects your thoughts, emotions, intentions, and spiritual vitality. Just as your body needs nourishment and care, so does your energetic field. Your aura is in constant dialogue with the world. It responds to people, environments, music, thoughts, and even your memories.

When your aura is strong and clear, you feel vibrant, confident, and spiritually connected. When it's weakened or cluttered, you may feel tired, anxious, heavy, or disconnected from your true self.

The Layers of the Aura

Most spiritual traditions recognize **seven layers** of the aura, each reflecting a deeper part of your being:

1. **Physical Layer** – Vitality, health, and physical comfort.

2. **Emotional Layer** – Feelings, sensitivity, moods.

3. **Mental Layer** – Thoughts, beliefs, mental clarity.

4. **Astral Layer** – Love, connection, relationship energy.

5. **Etheric Template** – Blueprint of your higher body.

6. **Celestial Layer** – Spiritual insight, divine guidance.

7. **Causal/Ketheric Layer** – Soul purpose, unity with source.

Each layer harmonizes with one of the chakras and collectively forms your **light body** — the energy vessel of your soul.

Clearing and Protecting Your Energy

Just as dust settles on a home, energy debris can collect in your aura — from negative interactions, stress, trauma, or even absorbing others' emotions. Regular energetic hygiene is essential for spiritual growth.

The Art of Smudging:

A Sacred Clearing Ritual

Purpose:

To clear stagnant, heavy, or negative energy from your aura or space. Smudging resets your energetic field and restores balance.

Tools Needed:

- Sage bundle, sweetgrass, or cedar.
- Palo santo.
- Clam shell or abalone shell.
- Feather or your hand for wafting.
- Matches or lighter.

Instructions:

1. Light your smudge stick until it smolders.
   Allow the sacred smoke to rise.
2. Begin at your heart, moving the smoke around your body—head to toe.
3. As you cleanse, say:
   "I release what is not mine. I return to my center. I call back my light."
4. When finished, extinguish the smudge safely. Offer gratitude to the plant spirits.

Note: Smudging is a sacred act. Always honor the traditions it stems from (especially Indigenous cultures), and use herbs ethically sourced.

Sensing Your Aura

You can begin to **feel or see** your aura with practice. Sit quietly with palms facing each other. Slowly move them apart and together. You may feel tingling, warmth, or resistance — this is your energy!

You can also gaze softly into a mirror with a neutral background. With relaxed vision, look just beyond your shoulder. You may begin to see color, glow, or light distortions — your aura in motion.

Ritual:
Aura Strengthening Visualization

Sit comfortably, feet on the ground, spine tall.
Close your eyes and breathe deeply.
Visualize a radiant white light surrounding you
like a cocoon.
With every inhale, imagine the light growing
brighter. With every exhale, release any
heaviness or static.

Affirm

*"I am a being of light. My energy is whole,
vibrant, and protected."*

Remain in this light for several minutes, then
gently return.

Journal Prompts

- When do I feel most energized and
  clear?
- What drains my energy or makes me
  feel heavy?
- How do I sense energy in others?
- What color or feeling does my aura
  have today?

Affirmation

*My aura is radiant, protected, and filled with
divine light. I release what no longer serves
me and return to my natural state of peace.*

Energy Reflections

_____

_____

_____

_____

_____

_____

_____

_____

_____

_____

 # Spirit Notes

_____

_____

_____

_____

_____

_____

_____

_____

_____

CHAPTER SIX: SPIRIT GUIDES, HIGHER GUIDES & SPIRIT ANIMALS

"We are never alone. Spirit walks with us, speaks to us, and shows up in forms both seen and unseen."

Opening Meditation:
Spirit Guides & Sacred Companions

"Meeting the Guides"

Find a quiet space and settle into stillness. Close your eyes and place your hands gently over your heart. Take a slow, deep breath in and exhale fully.

Imagine a soft mist parting before you, revealing the glowing presence of your guides—your spirit allies, animal messengers, and higher helpers. They have always walked beside you, and they greet you now with warmth and love.

Silently or aloud, say:
"I open my heart to divine connection. I welcome the presence of my spirit guides and sacred companions. Thank you for walking with me."

Breathe into this connection. Feel the comfort, the wisdom, the quiet recognition. When you are ready, begin the chapter—knowing you are not alone.

What Are Spirit Guides?

Spirit Guides are non-physical beings who walk with us from birth until our final breath—offering wisdom, protection, nudges, and unseen companionship.

These loving allies come from many realms and often have had lifetimes of their own. Some may have known us before, while others have been assigned to our soul's evolution.

Types of Spirit Guides:

- **Ancestors** – Those from your lineage who offer inherited wisdom and support.

- **Guardian Angels** – Celestial protectors who love unconditionally and watch over you.

- **Elemental Spirits** – Beings connected to Earth, Air, Fire, and Water.

- **Animal Messengers** – Creatures of instinct and spirit that teach, protect, and walk beside us

They may guide you through dreams, symbols, feelings, synchronicities, or sudden clarity. You do not have to *see* your guides to receive from them. They speak in the subtle language of the soul.

Who Are Higher Guides?

Higher Guides are luminous, multi-dimensional beings from elevated planes of consciousness. Their vibration is refined, transcendent, and deeply transformative. They are called in when your soul is ready to take quantum steps on the path.

Common Higher Guides Include:

- **Ascended Masters** (e.g., Quan Yin, Jesus, Mary Magdalene, St. Germain)

- **Archangels** (e.g., Michael for protection, Raphael for healing, Uriel for clarity)

- **Star Beings/Galactic Guides** – Teachers from other dimensional realms offering advanced wisdom

- **The Higher Self** – Your own divine essence, the soul-self that exists beyond time and ego.

These guides offer deep spiritual insight, soul remembrance, and energetic activations. Working with them requires discernment, clear intent, and the invitation of only that which serves your **highest good**.

How to Connect with Your Guides

- **Create a Sacred Space**: Light a candle, say a prayer, sit with your alter or sit by a tree.

- **Ask with Intention**: "Guide of light and love, I invite you into my awareness."

- **Watch for Synchronicities**: Repeating numbers, animal sightings, songs, dreams.
- **Trust What You Receive**: You may feel, hear, see, or just *know* their presence.

- **Keep a Spirit Journal**: Document messages, signs, or feelings.

What Are Spirit Animals?

Spirit Animals are sacred messengers who offer us guidance through instinct, energy, and symbolic meaning. They may appear in dreams, visions, meditations, or synchronistic real-world encounters.

Types of Spirit Animals:

- **Totem Animals** – Lifelong spiritual companions tied to your essence or soul path.

- **Power Animals** – Temporary helpers that walk with you during specific life phases or challenges.

- **Messenger Animals** – Brief but powerful appearances meant to deliver a clear message or signal a shift.

Spirit animals walk with shamans, medicine people, and spiritual seekers across cultures. They mirror your strengths, awaken hidden gifts, and remind you of your connection to nature and the unseen world.

Discovering Your Spirit Allies

You may already be aware of your spirit allies—or they may be waiting for you to notice. Begin by tuning into patterns and energy:

- Are there animals that have repeatedly appeared in your life?

- Have you ever felt a presence guiding or protecting you, especially in times of fear or change?

- Do certain names, places, or celestial symbols draw you in?

- In dreams, what beings do you see, and what do they say?

Visualization Practice: Meeting Your Spirit Guide or Animal

Find a quiet, comfortable space. Close your eyes and breathe deeply.

Visualize yourself walking through a forest, meadow, or temple. A being approaches you—a figure or animal that radiates warmth and light. Open your heart to this presence.

Ask its name. Ask why it has come.

Listen. Feel. Trust.

When ready, return and journal everything you remember.

Spirit Animal Mini Glossary
Top 20 Spirit Allies

- **Owl** – Inner wisdom, intuition, truth revealed in darkness

- **Butterfly** – Transformation, rebirth, lightness of being.

- **Bear** – Strength, grounding, introspection, healing.

- **Dolphin** – Joy, communication, emotional intelligence.

- **Lion** – Courage, nobility, personal power.

- **Wolf** – Loyalty, instinct, leadership within the tribe.

- **Eagle** – Divine sight, freedom, sacred purpose.

- **Horse** – Vital force, freedom, stamina, shamanic power.

- **Snake** – Shedding the old, kundalini energy, transformation.

- **Cat** – Independence, mystery, psychic sensitivity.

- **Fox** – Adaptability, cleverness, shape-shifter energy.

- **Turtle** – Patience, longevity, earth connection, ancient wisdom.

- **Crow** – Magic, prophecy, transformation between worlds.

- **Hummingbird** – Joy, resilience, lightness, heart energy.

- **Elephant** – Memory, devotion, family, divine strength.

- **Peacock** – Confidence, inner beauty, spiritual awakening.

- **Rabbit** – Fertility, creativity, fear transformed into flow.

- **Raven** – Deep mystery, messages from the beyond, change.

- **Bison** – Abundance, sacred prayer, earth blessing.

- **Dragonfly** – Illusion lifting, light codes, multidimensional sight.

Sacred Symbols & Their Energies

Symbol	*Meaning*
Spiral	Life-cycles, spiritual growth, the journey inward.
Lotus Flowers	Rising from darkness, divine awakening, purity.
Tree of Life	Interconnectedness of all life, Growth, lineage.

Ankh	Eternal life, divine balance Sacred breath of Spirit.
Feathers	Angelic message, lightness Spiritual freedom.
Chakra Wheels	Energy centers within the body, soul alignment.
Om (ॐ)	The sound of the Universe, sacred creation, unity.
Infinity (∞)	Timelessness, soul potential, limitlessness.
Butterfly	Symbol of transformation and beauty in transition.
(Third Eye)	Intuition, protection, deeper spiritual sight.
Sacred Geometry	Divine design, cosmic. order, pattern of creation. (Flower of life)

Ritual: Spirit Guide Invocation

You will need: A white candle, a quiet space, and a pen and paper.

Light the candle and center yourself with three slow meditation breaths. Place your hand over your heart and say aloud:

"I open my heart to the wisdom and love of my guides. Only those in alignment with the highest good may enter this space. I welcome the presence of my Spirit Guide, my Higher Guide, and my Spirit Animal. May I hear, feel, and trust your messages. I am ready."

Sit in silence for 5–10 minutes. Notice images, words, emotions, or physical sensations. Then, journal your experience with trust and curiosity.

Journal Prompts

- What energies or beings have I felt watching over me in this life?
- Which animals or archetypes appear often in my life?

- What do I feel or hear when I sit in quiet and ask for guidance?
- What kind of spiritual help do I desire most right now?

<u>Affirmation</u>

"I walk in harmony with the sacred ones who guide, protect, and awaken my soul."

Spirit Guide Journal

Spirit Guide Journal

 # Reflections

CHAPTER SEVEN:

ASTROLOGY –

THE LANGUAGE OF THE STARS

"As above, so below, as within, so without." – Hermetic Principle

What Is Astrology?

Astrology is the sacred art of interpreting the sky, the language of the stars-a sacred map that reveals how the cosmos imprints its energy upon our soul. It teaches us that the positions of the planets and stars at the moment of our birth reflect deep truths about who we are, why we're here, and how we grow.

It is not about prediction—but about understanding the deeper patterns, potentials, and lessons woven into your life path. Every planet, every sign, every celestial movement reflects a mirror of your inner world. Astrology shows us that we are not separate from the universe—we are deeply connected to it, born of its rhythm and wisdom.

Your birth chart, often called your natal chart, is a celestial blueprint. It is a guide that can illuminate your gifts, challenges, and soul's purpose. By understanding astrology, you begin to live more consciously, aligned with the natural cycles of life, and guided by the wisdom of the heavens.

Opening Meditation:

Astrology – The Language of the Stars

"Aligning with the Cosmos"

Sit quietly and close your eyes. Imagine yourself beneath a vast, star-filled sky. With each breath, feel the light of the stars pouring gently into your body—through the crown of your head, into your heart, and throughout your entire being.

You are stardust, woven from the same energy as the planets and constellations. You are part of the cosmic dance.

Whisper softly to yourself:
"I align with the rhythm of the universe. I open to the wisdom of the stars and the story they tell about my soul."

Invite your spirit guides and celestial allies to walk beside you as you explore the ancient language of astrology.

When you are ready, begin the chapter with wonder and reverence.

The Natal Chart: Your Soul's Blueprint

Your natal chart is a map of where all the planets were at the moment you were born. It shows the unique energy you were born into—your cosmic DNA.

- **Planets** = what energy is at play

- **Signs** = how that energy expresses itself

- **Houses** = where in your life that energy shows up

The Big Three: Sun, Moon & Rising

Sun Sign — Your Core Essence
The Sun shows your life purpose, identity, and creative life force.

The Moon – Your Reflection
The Moon reflects your emotions, intuition, and inner needs.

Rising Sign — Your Outer Self
The Rising Sign is how you appear to others and how you begin things.

The 12 Zodiac Signs

- **Aries** – Fire (Cardinal): Courage, action, leadership.

- **Taurus** – Earth (Fixed): Stability, sensuality, patience.

- **Gemini** – Air (Mutable): Curiosity, communication, learning.

- **Cancer** – Water (Cardinal): Nurturing, home, emotion.

- **Leo** – Fire (Fixed): Confidence, creativity, expression.

- **Virgo** – Earth (Mutable): Service, healing, detail.
- **Libra** – Air (Cardinal): Harmony, beauty, relationships.

- **Scorpio** – Water (Fixed): Depth, mystery, transformation.

- **Sagittarius** – Fire (Mutable): Freedom, truth, exploration.

- **Capricorn** – Earth (Cardinal): Ambition, structure, legacy.

- **Aquarius** – Air (Fixed): Innovation, community, vision.

- **Pisces** – Water (Mutable): Spirituality, dreams, compassion.

The 12 Houses of Life

- **1st House – Self**: Identity, appearance, beginnings.

- **2nd House – Value:** Money, self-worth, possessions.

- **3rd House – Communication:** Thinking, siblings, expression.

- **4th House – Home:** Roots, family, emotional base.

- **5th House – Creativity:** Joy, romance, personal expression.

- **6th House – Service:** Health, habits, daily life.

- **7th House – Relationships:** Partnerships, reflection.

- **8th House – Transformation:** Intimacy, death/rebirth, mystery.

- **9th House – Expansion:** Beliefs, travel, higher learning.

- **10th House – Career:** Purpose, reputation, achievement.

- **11th House – Community:** Friends, dreams, future vision.
- **12th House – Spirit:** Subconscious, endings, divine connection.

Planetary Archetypes (Beginner's Glossary)

- ☉ **Sun** – Identity, self, life force.
- ☽ **Moon** – Emotions, inner world, intuition.
- ☿ **Mercury** – Thought, communication, intellect.
- ♀ **Venus** – Love, beauty, value.
- ♂ **Mars** – Action, passion, courage.
- ♃ **Jupiter** – Expansion, blessings, wisdom.
- ♄ **Saturn** – Structure, responsibility, growth.
- ♅ **Uranus** – Change, freedom, awakening.
- ♆ **Neptune** – Dreams, illusion, spirit.
- ♇ **Pluto** – Power, transformation, depth.
- ⚷ **Chiron** – Wounding, soul healing, gift.
- ☊ **North Node** – Growth, life direction.
- ☋ **South Node** – Past life patterns, karmic gifts.

Understanding the Chart as a Whole

Your chart is not a list of separate signs and symbols—it is a sacred symphony of energies working together.

You are not just your Sun sign. You are a unique combination of:

- Planetary forces
- Expressed through signs
- Playing out in houses

Astrology helps you:

- Understand your gifts
- Navigate challenges
- Align with divine timing
- Grow into your highest self

Your chart is a map of your becoming.

Ritual: Blessing Your Birth Chart

You'll need: your printed chart, a white candle, and a crystal.

1. Light the candle and place your hand over your chart.

2. Say: *"I bless this sacred map of my soul. May I understand its truth and honor its design."*

3. Place the crystal at the center and breathe.

4. Journal what you feel or intuitively receive.

Journal Prompts

- How do I feel when I look at the stars or moon?
- Which part of my Big Three do I relate to most?
- How can astrology help me love myself more fully?

Affirmation

"I am a divine spark of the cosmos, born of stardust and purpose. The stars guide me home to myself."

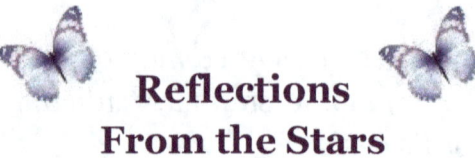

Reflections
From the Stars

_____

_____

_____

_____

_____

_____

_____

_____

_____

_____

Reflections From
the Stars

Reflections

_____

CHAPTER EIGHT:

MOON WISDOM: WORKING WITH

THE PHASES OF THE MOON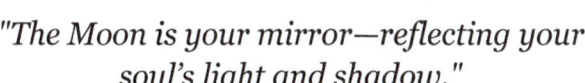

*"The Moon is your mirror—reflecting your
soul's light and shadow."*

What Is Moon Wisdom?

Moon Wisdom is the sacred practice of
attuning your life to the rhythms of the Moon.
For centuries, spiritual seekers, priestesses,
and earth-based traditions have looked to the
Moon as a guide—a mirror of inner tides and
emotional truth. Just as the Moon waxes and
wanes in the sky, we too move through cycles
of growth, release, reflection, and renewal.
Moon Wisdom teaches us that timing
matters, that stillness has value, and that our
intuition is strongest when we honor the
natural flow of energy. By observing the
Moon's phases—New Moon, Waxing, Full,
Waning—we begin to understand our own
needs, desires, and inner transformations.

Living by Moon Wisdom means living in
harmony with nature, our spirit, and the
divine feminine. It is an invitation to
reconnect with the sacred pulse of the
universe through the gentle light of the Moon.

Opening Meditation: Moon Wisdom

"In Rhythm with the Moon"

Close your eyes and breathe deeply, imagining soft moonlight cascading over your body. Let the light wrap around you like a silvery blanket—cool, calm, and luminous.

Feel yourself in rhythm with the tides, your breath rising and falling like waves under a full moon.

Whisper gently to yourself:
"I open to the wisdom of the Moon. I honor her phases within me—times of stillness, growth, release, and renewal."

Call upon the Moon Goddess, your lunar guides, and the sacred feminine to guide this chapter. When you feel aligned, begin.

New Moon Intention & New Beginnings

Energy: Stillness, planting seeds, going inward
Rituals:

- Write new moon intentions.
- Charge crystals with purpose.
- Begin a new project or journal cycle.

Affirmation:
"I plant seeds of magic and trust in divine timing."

Waxing Moon
Growth & Momentum

Energy: Expansion, taking action, building power.

Rituals:

- Take steps toward your goal.
- Practice visualizations.
- Do energizing breathwork.

Affirmation:
"I grow with grace and strength."

Full Moon
Illumination & Release

Energy: Culmination, celebration, emotional clarity.

Rituals:

- Fire bowl or burning ritual.
- Cleanse aura or space with water or smoke.
- Journal what you are ready to release.

Affirmation:
"I release what no longer serves and make room for light."

Waning Moon
Surrender & Rest

Energy: *Letting go, forgiveness, integration*
Rituals:

- Salt bath and dream journaling.
- Forgiveness practices.
- Cord-cutting visualization.

Affirmation: *"I surrender and trust the flow of life."*

Dark Moon
Deep Rest & Void Wisdom

Energy: *Mystery, retreat, soul listening*
Rituals:

- Meditate in silence or darkness.
- Ask Spirit for guidance.
- Pull oracle or tarot cards.

Affirmation: *"In the void, I remember my truth."*

Journal Prompts:

- What is rising to the surface for me this full moon?
- What am I ready to call in under this new moon?

How does my energy shift during each lunar phase?

Optional Moon aspects

- 🌕 *March 14 and September 7 are* eclipses — powerful moments of transformation.
- 🌑 Use the New Moon for intention setting.
- 🌕 Use the Full Moon for release and   healing.
- 🌗 The Last Quarter invites reflection and integration.
  🌙 Moon Ritual Companion: 2025–2027
  Use this page for marking moon phases and ritual planning. Circle each New, First Quarter, Full, and Last Quarter Moon as it rises in your skies.

2025 Moon Phases

New Moon	First Qtr.	Full Moon	Last Qtr.
Jan 29	Feb 5	Jan 13	Feb 20
Feb 27	Mar 6	Feb 12	Mar 22
Mar 29	Apr 4	Mar 14 L. Eclipse	Apr 20
Apr 27	May 4	Apr 12	May20

2025 Moon Phases Cont.

New Moon	First Qtr.	Full Moon	Last Qtr.
May 26	Jun 2	May 12	June 18
June 25	July 2	June 11	July 18
July 24	Aug 1	July 10	Aug 16
Aug 23	Aug 30	Aug 9	Sept 15
Sep 21	Sep 28	Sep 7 L Eclipse	Oct 14
Oct 21	Oct 29	Oct 6	Nov 13
Nov 20	Nov 27	Nov 5	Dec 12

2026 Moon Phases Cont.

New Moon	First Qtr.	Full Moon	Last Qtr.
Jan 18	Jan 25	Feb 1	Feb 10
Feb 17	Feb 24	Mar 3 L. Eclipse	Mar 12
Mar 19	Mar 26	Apr 2	Apr 10
Apr 17	Apr 23	May 1	May 9
May 16	May 23	May 31	June 8
June 15	June 21	June 29	July 7
July 14	July 20	July 29	Aug 6
Aug 13	Aug 20	Aug 28 Eclipse	Sept 4
Sep 12	Sep 18	Sep 26	Oct 2
Oct 11	Oct 18	Oct 26	Nov 3
Nov 9	Nov 16	Nov 24	Dec 2

2027 Moon Phases

New Moon	First Qtr.	Full Moon	Last Qtr.
Jan 7	Jan 15	Jan 22	Jan 29
Feb 6	Feb 14	Feb 20 Eclipse	Feb 28
Mar 8	Mar 15	Mar 22	Mar 30
Apr 7	Apr 12	Apr 20	Apr 28
May 6	May 13	May 20	May 28
June 4	June 11	June19	June 27
July 4	July 11	July 18	July 26
Aug 2	Aug 9	Aug 17	Aug 25
Sep 1	Sep 7	Sept 15	Sept 23
Oct 1	Oct 7	Oct 15	Oct 22
Nov 6	Nov 14	Nov 21	Nov 28

Ritual Notes & Guidance

Eclipses:

Mar 14, 2025 (Full Moon): Total Lunar Eclipse — a powerful time for deep emotional release

Sep 7, 2025 (Full Moon): Total Lunar Eclipse — a moment of transformation

Feb 20, 2027 (Full Moon): Penumbral Lunar Eclipse — ideal for spiritual insight

- **New Moon:** Set new intentions and plant spiritual seeds.

- **First Quarter:** Take inspired action and momentum.

- **Full Moon:** Celebrate, release, heal, and complete.

- **Last Quarter:** Reflect, integrate, and rest.

New Moon Intentions

_____

_____

_____

_____

_____

_____

_____

_____

_____

_____

Full Moon Release

Reflections

CHAPTER NINE:
TAROT & SACRED NUMBERS

"The cards do not predict the future—they reveal the soul's present conversation with the universe."

What Is the Tarot?

Tarot is a sacred mirror of the soul—a deck of 78 symbolic cards that offer insight, reflection, and guidance. More than a tool for fortune-telling, the Tarot is a language of archetypes and universal truths that speak to the depths of our inner world. Each card, from the mysterious Fool to the luminous Star, tells a story—a journey of growth, challenge, transformation, and spiritual awakening. The Tarot doesn't give answers; it opens doors. It invites you to listen, reflect, and trust your intuition as you explore your life's path. Whether used for personal discovery, daily insight, or divine connection, the Tarot is a trusted companion that helps you make sense of life's mysteries. It is a sacred portal that blends the wisdom of the cosmos with the whisper of your inner voice.

Opening Meditation: Tarot & Numerology

"Opening the Portal of Symbols"

Sit in stillness and gently close your eyes.
With each breath, imagine stepping into a sacred inner temple— lit by candles and filled with ancient symbols.
Around you shimmer the energies of numbers, archetypes, and cards—each one holding a key to deeper wisdom.
Invite your higher self and your spirit team to guide you now.

Whisper softly:

"I open my heart to receive guidance through symbols and numbers. I trust the messages of Spirit that flow through the Tarot and the sacred language of numerology."

Breathe, receive, and when you feel ready, begin the chapter with open eyes and a listening soul.

The Tarot Deck - The deck is divided into:

- 22 Major Arcana: The soul's journey through universal truths
- 56 Minor Arcana: Daily life lessons, divided into four suits (Cups, Pentacles, Swords, and Wands)

The Tarot allows you to hear what your soul already knows.

What Is Numerology?

Numerology is the mystical study of numbers and their sacred meanings. Numerology becomes a guiding compass, helping you step more fully into your soul's purpose with understanding, intention, and grace.
It teaches that numbers are not just quantities—they are vibrations, energies, and cosmic codes that shape our personalities, life paths, and soul contracts. Every number holds a frequency that speaks to a deeper truth: who you are, why you are here, and what lessons you are meant to learn. From your birthdate to the letters in your name, Numerology reveals patterns that illuminate your strengths, challenges, and divine timing. Like a hidden map, it offers clarity in times of confusion and confidence in moments of choice. In harmony with the Tarot.

Numerology in the Tarot

Numbers hold vibration, intention, and cosmic meaning. In Tarot, numbers offer an added layer of wisdom:

- They provide structure to the cards.
- They deepen meaning across both Major and Minor Arcana.
- They help you recognize spiritual patterns.

Meaning of Numbers 1–10 in Tarot

1	New beginnings, initiative	The Magician, Ace of Wands
2	Duality, Balance choices	High Priestess Two of Cups
3	Creativity, expansion	The Empress Three of Disks
4	Foundation, stability	The Emperor, Four of Swords
5	Change, growth Challenge,	The Hierphant Five of Wands
6	Harmony, healing, unity	The Lovers Six of Cups
7	Mystery, introspection	The Chariot, Seven of Sword
8	Power, mastery movement	Strength, Eight of Disks
9	Completion, wisdom	The Hermit Nine of Wands
10	Fulfillment, transformation	Wheel of Fortune Ten of Cups

Major Arcana: The Soul's Journey

The Major Arcana tells the mythic story of The Fool, the soul, journeying through life lessons from 0 to 21:

- The Fool (0): Innocence, trust, the leap of faith

- The Magician (1): Willpower, manifestation

- The High Priestess (2): Intuition, mystery

    ...and so on through:

- The World (21): Completion, unity, cosmic understanding

Each card represents an archetype we all experience. Drawing one invites you to explore how that energy is moving in your life.

Numerology & the Soul Cycle

Numerology, like Tarot, is a mystical system to understand your soul's blueprint. Three powerful teachings include:

Life Path Number
(Your Soul's Purpose)

Add your full birth date and reduce it to a single digit or master number.

Example: February 20, 1962
$2 + 2 + 0 + 1 + 9 + 6 + 2 = 22$
Master Number: 22 – The Master Builder
You are here to turn divine inspiration into form and build for the greater good.

Growth Cycles
Based on month, day, and year of birth:

- **Formative Cycle** (birth to ~35): February = 2 → Peace, intuition, emotional strength

- **Productive Cycle** (~35 to ~60): 20 = Diplomacy, relationships, balance

- **Harvest Cycle** (60+): 1962 = 1 + 9 + 6 + 2 = 18 → 9 → Wisdom, service, completion

These cycles reveal the evolving focus of your spiritual development.

Personal Year Number

Use your birth month + day + current year.

Step 1: Birth Month + Day
February 20 → 2 + 2 + 0 = 4

Step 2: Add to the Universal Year
2025 → 2 + 0 + 2 + 5 = 9

4 + 9 = 13 → This is your Personal Year Number

Personal Year 13 =

Transformation Through Structure
The number 13 is not unlucky—it is sacred. It brings a powerful shift that requires shedding old skins to rebuild something stronger.

This is a karmic year of deep transformation, responsibility, and spiritual reorganization.

You are asked to lay down new spiritual or physical foundations with wisdom earned from the past.

Theme: Endings, rebirth, restructuring, self-discipline, breaking outdated patterns.

Interpreting the Numbers in Practice

Ask: "What number is appearing repeatedly for me right now?"

- In Tarot spreads
- In birthdays or dates
- In years or cycles

Each number calls you to reflect on its lesson.

Ritual: One-Card Daily Draw

1. Sit in silence. Breathe deeply.
2. Ask: "What energy or insight do I need today?"
3. Shuffle and draw one card.
4. Reflect on its number, suit, and image.
5. Journal your message.

Over time, you will notice patterns and themes speaking to your soul.

Journal Prompts

- What number appears in my life again and again?

- What card do I most resonate with right now?

- What lesson am I meant to master in this personal year?

Affirmation

"I trust the sacred language of numbers and cards to reveal what my soul is ready to learn. I am always guided."

Messages from the Cards

_____

_____

_____

_____

_____

_____

_____

_____

_____

_____

Messages from the Numbers

_____

_____

_____

_____

_____

_____

_____

_____

_____

Reflection Journal

THE
CHAKRA
SYSTEM

CHAPTER TEN:
THE CHAKRAS

"You are not just a body—you are energy in motion, light in form."

What Are Chakras?

Your chakras are the sacred rainbow bridges between your body and spirit. The chakra system is an ancient map of the body's subtle energy centers, passed down through yogic and spiritual traditions for thousands of years. "Chakra" is a Sanskrit word meaning "wheel" or "disc," and each chakra is seen as a spinning vortex of life force energy that governs different aspects of your physical, emotional, mental, and spiritual well-being.

There are seven primary chakras aligned along the spine, from the Root at the base to the Crown at the top of the head. Each chakra vibrates with a unique color and frequency, and each one influences how you feel, connect, and express yourself in the world.

When your chakras are balanced and open, energy flows freely, and you feel grounded, inspired, confident, loving, expressive, intuitive, and spiritually connected. When blocked or imbalanced, these areas of life may feel stuck, heavy, or out of sync.

Learning about the chakra system empowers you to care for your energy field with intention—through meditation, breathwork, sound, movement, color, affirmations, and ritual.

The chakras are more than just spiritual theory-they are living gateways of transformation that help you bridge your body and soul. As you awaken each one, you step more fully into your truth, wholeness, and divine light.

Opening Meditation:
The Chakra System

"Aligning the Energy Body"

Sit quietly and take a few deep breaths. Bring your awareness to the base of your spine. Imagine a glowing red light there—warm, steady, grounding. As you breathe, allow this light to rise gently upward, activating and illuminating each energy center:

💗 **Red at the Root** – grounding and safety

🧡 **Orange at the Sacral** – creativity and emotion

💛 **Yellow** at the Solar Plexus – confidence and will

💚 **Green** at the Heart – love and compassion

💙 **Blue** at the Throat – truth and expression

💜 **Indigo** at the Third Eye – intuition and insight

🤍 **Violet** or White at the Crown – connection to source.

Feel this rainbow of energy flowing freely through you, cleansing, balancing, and awakening your inner light.

"I align my energy with light, love, and truth. Welcome the wisdom of my chakras and the healing they bring."

Rest in this glow… and when you feel harmonized, begin the chapter.

The Seven Chakras in Detail

Chakra	Color	Loc.	Crystals	Scent /Oils
Root	Red	Spine Base	Hematite, Jasper, Smoky Qtz	Patchouli Cedarwood
Sacral	Orange	Lower Abdomen	Carnelian, Moonstone Calcite	Sandalwood Ylang Ylang Sweet Orange
Solar Plexus	Yellow	Upper Abdomen	Yellow Jasper Tiger's Eye Citrine	Lemon Ginger Chamomile
Heart	Green Pink	Chest	Rose Qtz Aventurine. Emerald	Eucalyptus Geranium Rose
Throat	Lt. Blue	Neck	Lapis Lazuli Aquamarine Bl. Lace Agate	Peppermint Eucalyptus Frankincense
Mind's Eye	Dk Blue	Forehead Eye Brows	Sodalite Amethyst Fluorite	Clary Sage Lavender Mugwort
Crown	Violet or White	Top Of Head	Clear Qtz Selenite Amethyst	Lotus Frankincense Myrrh

Chakra Affirmations

- **Root:** "I am safe, grounded, and connected to the Earth."
- **Sacral:** "I embrace my emotions and creative flow."
- **Solar Plexus:** "I honor my personal power and inner strength."
- **Heart:** "I give and receive love with ease and grace."
- **Throat:** "I express my truth clearly and confidently."
- **Third Eye:** "I trust my intuition and inner vision."
- **Crown:** "I am one with divine light and universal wisdom."

Emotional Patterns (Balanced vs. Blocked)

Chakra	Balanced State	Blocked Expression
Root	Grounded, secure, trusting	Fear, anxiety, instability
Sacral	Joyful, creative, emotionally open	Shame, guilt creative blocks
Solar Plexus	Confident, empowered Decisive	Low self-esteem anger, control issues

Chakra	Balanced State	Blocked Expression
Heart	Compassionate, forgiving, open-hearted	Jealousy, grief, emotional walls
Throat	Honest, expressive, good communicator	Silence, fear of speaking up
Minds (3rd) Eye	Intuitive, visionary clear-minded	Confusion, denial, overthinking
Crown	Spiritually connected, peaceful	Disconnected, cynical, spiritual apathy

Aura & Energy Field

Your aura is the luminous field of energy that surrounds your body. It reflects your mood, health, and spiritual vibration.

Your chakras feed into the aura, influencing its color and clarity. When your chakras are clear, your aura glows with radiant hues. When blocked, your aura may feel heavy, cloudy, or "off."

Aura Color Meanings (simplified)

- **Red** – Vitality, passion, drive
- **Orange** – Creativity, joy, emotional energy
- **Yellow** – Confidence, intellect, clarity
- **Green** – Healing, compassion, growth
- **Blue** – Truth, peace, communication
- **Indigo** – Intuition, insight, inner knowing
- **White/Violet** – Spiritual wisdom, enlightenment

Energy Hygiene Practices

Maintaining your energy field is as essential as physical self-care.

- Smudging with sage, palo santo, or herbs
- Salt baths or foot soaks
- Energy brushing: sweep your hands down your aura to clear it
- Visualization: imagine white light cleansing your field
- Crystals: carry chakra stones or wear them as jewelry
- Sound: Use singing bowls, mantras, or tuning forks

Chakra Alignment Meditation (Ritual)

1. Sit or lie down in a quiet space.
2. Place a crystal for each chakra on your body (optional).
3. Breathe deeply. With each breath, imagine a glowing ball of colored light at each chakra.
4. Chant or listen to the Bija mantras as you move from Root to Crown.
5. Feel the balance and alignment restoring your energy body.

Closing Affirmation

"My energy flows freely. I honor each center of my being with love, light, and compassion. I am aligned, balanced, and whole."

Mini Chakra Self-Assessment Quiz

Which chakra needs attention?

Answer Yes or No to these:

- Do I feel ungrounded, anxious, or disconnected from my body? → Root

- Do I struggle with pleasure, intimacy, or creativity? → Sacral

- Do I feel powerless or unmotivated? → Solar Plexus

- Do I have difficulty giving or receiving love? → Heart

- Do I avoid expressing myself or feel unheard? → Throat

- Do I ignore my intuition or feel mentally scattered? → Third Eye

- Do I feel disconnected from purpose or spirit? → Crown

The more "Yes" responses in one row, the more that chakra may need attention.

Chakra Reflections

_____

_____

_____

_____

_____

_____

_____

_____

_____

_____

_____

_____

Energy Notes

Reflections

CHAPTER ELEVEN: EARTH MAGIC & RITUAL

"The Earth is not just our home—She is a living temple. When we honor her, she awakens something ancient within us."

What Is Earth Magic?

Earth Magic is the ancient practice of working in harmony with the natural world to create healing, intention, and transformation It is the remembering that all of life is sacred—that stones carry stories, herbs hold wisdom, the moon speaks in phases, and fire listens when we speak our truth. Earth Magic isn't about spells or superstition it's about relationship. It's about honoring the energy of the land, the cycles of the seasons, and the spirit that lives in all things. Through rituals, offerings, sacred tools, and intentional acts, Earth Magic helps us reconnect with the rhythms of nature and the divine presence woven throughout it. When we align with the Earth in this sacred way, we remember that we are not separate from the magic—we *are* the magic. The Earth becomes both altar and ally, guiding us back to our intuition, creativity, and power.

Opening Meditation: Earth Magic & Ritual

"Rooted in the Sacred"

Sit quietly and bring your awareness to the Earth beneath you.

Imagine roots extending from your body into the soil, anchoring you deeply into the heart of the Earth. Feel the steady, ancient energy rising up to meet you—warm, nourishing, alive.

Around you, the elements gather: Earth, Air, Fire, Water, and Spirit. They greet you as kin.

Whisper softly:

"I honor the sacred magic of the Earth. I open my heart to her rhythms, her wisdom, and her power to heal and transform."

Feel the presence of the natural world surrounding you. The stones, trees, herbs, winds, and moonlight—all part of your ritual family.

When you are grounded and open, begin the chapter with reverence.

The Four Elements in Ritual

Element	Symbol	Direction	Ritual Use
Earth	Soil Stones,	North	Grounding, Stability Abundance Manifestation
Water	Bowl Shells	West	Emotion Intuition Cleansing Healing
Fire	Candle, ember,	South	passion, Transformation courage Purification
Air	Feather incense	East	Clarity, wisdom communication breath of spirit

You can invoke all four elements in a ritual circle to call balance and harmony.

Working with the Moon

- New Moon – Set intentions, plant seeds

- Waxing Moon – Take inspired action, growth

- Full Moon – Celebrate, release, amplify energy
- Waning Moon – Cleanse, let go, rest

Ritual - Create a moon water jar under a full moon. Use it to anoint your altar, plants, or your third eye during meditation.

Simple Earth-Based Rituals

1. Barefoot Grounding
Stand with bare feet on the Earth. Breathe deeply. Imagine roots growing from your feet into the soil. Say:

"I root myself in the wisdom of the Earth. I am safe, whole, and supported."

2. Seasonal Altar Offering
Offer dried herbs, seeds, or flowers from each season to your altar. Whisper gratitude to the Earth.

3. Stone Circle for Protection
Create a circle of stones around your meditation space or bed. Each stone becomes a guardian.

4. Fire Release Ceremony
Write down what you're releasing. Burn the paper in a safe fire bowl, saying: "With fire, I transform. I let go. I rise anew."

Sacred Tools of Earth Magic

Tool	*Use*
Salt	Purification, protection, grounding
Herbs	Healing, spell work, smoke cleansing (e.g., rosemary, sage, lavender)

Crystals - Energetic support, amplification, chakra healing.

Feathers - Air connection, blessing energy, clearing space.

Flowers - Devotion, heart energy, seasonal cycles.

Jars & - Intention magic, herb storage,
Bottles moon, water.

Earth Magic Blessing

Stand under the open sky, place your hands on your heart and say:
"With the wind in my breath, the fire in my soul, the water of my heart, and the Earth beneath my feet I honor all that is sacred. I walk in balance. I remember who I am."

Journal Prompts

- When do I feel closest to the Earth?
- What sacred places in nature hold meaning for me?
- How can I honor the Earth through my everyday rituals?

Affirmation

"I am one with the Earth. Her wisdom flows through me. Her cycles are my guide."

Natures Whispers

Earth Notes

_____

_____

_____

_____

_____

_____

_____

_____

_____

Awareness Notes

CHAPTER TWELVE:

LISTENING TO YOUR THE INNER VOICE

"The soul speaks in whispers. Listen with your heart."

What Is the Inner Voice?

Your inner voice is the sacred whisper of your soul. It is the quiet, wise presence within you that gently guides, nudges, and speaks the truth—even when the world is loud and your mind may not yet understand. Unlike fear, ego, or external noise, the inner voice doesn't shout. It speaks softly through feelings, knowing, imagery, or quiet phrases that arise without effort. This voice is the language of your Higher Self, of Spirit working through you. It may come in stillness, in nature, through writing, or in moments when you are simply being instead of doing.

Listening to your inner voice means learning to trust yourself. It's not about perfection or always having the right answer—it's about cultivating a sacred relationship with your inner knowing.

The more you listen, the stronger and clearer it becomes. Honoring this voice is a radical act of self-love, authenticity, and spiritual alignment. In a world full of noise, your inner voice is a compass guiding you back to your truth. It speaks in peace, not pressure. It is the voice of your higher self— the divine spark within you.

You may also know it as:

- Intuition
- Soul wisdom
- Inner knowing
- Spirit guidance
- The voice of love

Opening Meditation: Listening to Your Inner Voice

"The Whisper Within"
Sit quietly and bring your hands to your heart. Breathe slowly and deeply, allowing your breath to soften the mind and quiet the noise around you.

With each inhale, draw your awareness inward. With each exhale, release any doubt, fear, or distraction. Imagine a soft light glowing at the center of your chest—a light that pulses with your soul's truth.

Whisper softly to yourself:
"I am listening. I trust the voice of my soul. I welcome clarity, truth, and gentle wisdom from within."

Rest here in stillness. Trust what rises. Know that your inner voice is sacred—it speaks not in volume, but in truth.

When you are ready, begin this chapter with an open heart.

How to Tell the Difference: Fear vs. Intuition

Intuition *(Inner Voice)*	Fear *(Mind Noise)*
Calm, clear, steady	Anxious, racing, urgent
Comes in softly	Shouts or panics
Rooted in love	Rooted in lack or control
Knows what's right	Worries about being wrong
Present moment clarity	Future-focused obsession

Practice Tip: If it feels like pressure— it's not your inner voice.

Daily Practices to Connect with Your Inner Voice

1. Stillness Practice

Sit quietly for 5–10 minutes. Place one hand on your heart and the other on your belly. Breathe slowly. **Ask aloud:**

"What truth do I need to hear today?"
Listen without trying to answer. Let the whisper rise.

2. Soul Writing

Write a question at the top of a journal page:
"Dear Inner Voice, what would you like me to know?"

Then allow the pen to move. Don't judge what comes. Let the voice of your soul speak.

3. Sacred Yes / Sacred No Exercise

Think of a joyful memory and feel what a YES feels like in your body.

Then recall something you regret or avoided—that's your NO feeling.

"Your body is the sacred compass of your soul. Learn how it says yes and no, and you'll never be lost again."

Listening Ritual: Candle of Clarity

Light a white or blue candle. Sit in stillness and say:

"I call upon my higher self, my Spirit Guides, and Divine Wisdom. May the voice of my soul rise above all fear and distraction.

I am ready to listen."
Then ask your question and listen with your full presence.

Journal Prompts

- When have I listened to my inner voice—and been glad I did?
- What does intuition feel like in my body?
- What blocks me from trusting myself more fully?
- What would change if I let my soul lead?

Affirmation

"My inner voice is wise, loving, and always guiding me home. I trust the sacred whisper within."

Messages from My
Divine Guide

_____

_____

_____

_____

_____

_____

_____

_____

_____

_____

Divine Inspiration

CHAPTER THERTEEN: RITUALS OF RELEASE & RENEWAL

"Let go with love. Begin again with light."

What Are Rituals of Release & Renewal?

Rituals of release and renewal are sacred acts of letting go and beginning again. They honor the natural cycles of life, where endings make space for new beginnings, and were clearing away the old allows our soul to breathe. These rituals are not about forgetting the past—they are about acknowledging what no longer serves us, offering it gratitude, and setting it free. Through symbolic actions like writing, burning, smudging, bathing, or speaking aloud, we give form to the inner desire to shed, shift, and start anew.

Renewal is the sacred return to the self. It is the quiet rebirth that follows release—the moment when your heart feels light again, when inspiration stirs, and when hope returns like spring after winter.

These rituals remind us that we are never stuck, never too late, and always capable of transformation.

When practiced with intention and care, rituals of release and renewal become portals of healing—restoring our clarity, our trust, and our radiant sense of possibility.

Opening Meditation: Rituals of Release & Renewal

"Breathing Out the Old, Breathing in the New"

Sit quietly and allow your breath to deepen. With each exhale, imagine releasing what no longer serves you—old thoughts, heavy emotions, patterns ready to fall away.

With each inhale, draw in fresh energy—light, clarity, and renewal.

Visualize a gentle wind blowing through you, clearing the inner landscape like leaves being swept from a forest path.

Whisper softly:
"I release with love. I welcome renewal. I trust the cycles of death and rebirth within me."

As you breathe, feel space opening inside you—a sacred space ready to be filled with new dreams, intentions, and light.

When your heart feels clear and calm, begin the chapter with reverence.

Why We Release

To walk a spiritual path is to understand that we are constantly evolving—and with each step, we are invited to let go of what no longer serves our highest good.

Holding onto something that no longer serves you is to close your hands to the blessings waiting to arrive. Releasing is not forgetting or rejecting—it is choosing freedom, growth, and alignment with your soul's truth.

We release to:

- Unbind from the past
- Clear energetic residue
- Make space for renewal and rebirth
- Honor endings as sacred thresholds
- Habits and patterns that keep us small
- Emotions we've carried to long
- Energies that don't belong to us
- Relationships, identities, fears, and even dreams that were part of a former chapter of you

Release is not a failure.

It is a sacred act of self-respect and soul alignment. It's saying, *"I trust who I am becoming more than I fear what I am leaving behind."*
When we release, we make space.
Space for new beginnings.
Space for joy.
Space for Spirit to flow freely through us again.

Just as the trees drop their leaves each autumn—not in despair, but in wisdom—so too must we shed what has run its course.

"Release is an offering. A spiritual surrender. A promise that we will not carry what was never ours to hold."

Through ritual, we give form to this sacred act. Whether we write it down and burn it, speak it into the wind, or bury it into the Earth, release becomes a ceremony of renewal—and we emerge lighter, clearer, and ready.

When to Practice Release & Renewal

- At the **Full Moon** (culmination and release)
- During **seasonal shifts** (Equinoxes, Solstices)
- At the end of a life chapter, relationship, or healing cycle
- When your body or spirit feels heavy, cluttered, or stuck

Rituals for Release

1. Fire Bowl Ceremony
Write what you wish to release on small slips of paper. Light a candle. Burn each slip safely in a bowl, saying:

"I release this with love. I am free. So, it is."

2. Salt Bath Purification
Add Sea salt and lavender to a warm bath. As you soak, imagine heaviness dissolving from your body. Drain the water with gratitude and say:

"With this water, I release what I no longer carry."

3.Cord Cutting Visualization
Visualize a cord connecting you to a person, pattern, or fear. Ask Archangel Michael or your higher self to cut the cord with love and light. Breathe deeply.

Rituals for Renewal

1. Planting a Seed
Hold a physical seed or symbolic object. Whisper your new intention into it. Plant it in soil. As it grows, so does your new path.

2. New Moon Water Blessing
Under the New Moon, bless a jar of water
with your wishes. Drink a little each day,
reminding yourself of your renewal.

3. Breath of Renewal
Breathe in light. Hold it. Breathe out release.
Do this 7 times with the mantra:

"I breathe in clarity. I breathe out what no
longer serves."

<u>Chapter Affirmation</u>

"I trust in the wisdom of letting go. I make
space for what is true and new."

Tear-Out/ Pull-Out for
Chapter 13:
Letting Go & Starting Anew

Soul Guidance – "The Courage to Release, the Grace to Begin Again"

Letting go is not forgetting. It is honoring what has been, and then lovingly setting it free.

Whether you're releasing an old wound, a worn-out belief, a version of yourself, or a season of your life—know this: release is a sacred act of love. You are not losing something—you are making space for something more aligned.

This is your spiritual permission slip to say: "This no longer belongs to me."

Letting go can feel like grief, like fear, like freedom. There is no right way. Just your way. Some seasons close quietly. Others fall like towers. But each ending carries the seed of a new beginning.

Guidance for Release:

- Take a breath. Feel into what your body is holding on to.
- Ask: *What am I ready to release, forgive, or surrender?*
- Write it down. Speak it aloud. Burn it, bury it, or bless it.
- Let it leave your hands with love.

Pg. 126

Encouragement for New Beginnings:

- Every release creates room for renewal.

- Your next chapter doesn't need to be perfect—it just needs to be true.

- Start with small sacred steps: a new affirmation, a gentle boundary, a soul-aligned "yes."

- The Universe meets your courage with grace.

- You don't have to know the whole path—just the next lighted step.

"You are not behind. You are exactly where your soul needs you to be"

Ritual Reflection Page – "Release & Renew"

What I Am Releasing:

_____

_____

_____

_____

_____

What I Am Grateful for From This Experience

My Soul's New Beginning Looks Like:

Journal Prompts

- What am I ready to release—gently and completely?

- What is my spirit asking me to make space for?

- What has been a blessing in disguise that I now lay to rest?

Affirmation:

"I release with love. I welcome what is meant for me. I walk forward in light."

Optional Ritual:

Write your release list on a separate piece of paper and use fire (burn), earth (bury), or water (dissolve) to complete your ritual. Close with a blessing and gratitude.

What I Am Ready
To Release

My Sacred Renewal

What I Am Ready to Release
Extra pages

 # My Sacred Renewal
Extra Pages

_____

_____

_____

_____

_____

_____

_____

_____

_____

_____

_____

_____

CHAPTER FOURTEEN: EMBODIED LIGHT

"You are not here to chase the light. You are here to become it."

What Does It Mean to Embody the Light?

Embodied Light is the practice of **living your spiritual truth** —not just in quiet moments of reflection, but in the everyday unfolding of your life. It is the radiant integration of all you have remembered, healed, and reclaimed on your spiritual path. You no longer reach for the light outside yourself— you recognize it is within yourself and allow it to shine through your words, choices, presence, and purpose.

It is not just a state of being—it is a way of living.

When you embody the light:

- You Love with awareness
- You speak with kindness
- You act with courage and compassion
- You listen deeply to your intuition
- You move with reverence
- You create with purpose
- You radiate peace even when the world feels chaotic
- You heal through presence

You are not separate from the light—you are the vessel for it.

Embodying the light is a practice of being fully alive, grounded in love, and aligned with your soul's essence.

It does not mean perfection. It means presence. It means being honest, heart-centered, and spiritually awake in how you move through the world. Every act of compassion, every moment of authenticity, every breath of awareness becomes part of your lightwork.

This chapter is not an end—it is a beginning. A reminder that your light is needed. And that your life, lived with intention and grace, is the most powerful form of magic.

To embody the light is to become a living altar:

- You honor your body as sacred.
- You honor your emotions as guides.
- You honor your experiences as lessons.
- You honor your soul as your compass.

You begin to *glow from within.*
Not because life is easy—but because you
have remembered who you truly are:
A spark of the divine. A vessel of love. A
beacon for others.

**"You are not just here to seek the
light. You are here to become it."**

And so, to embody the light is to say:

- I choose love, again and again.

- I will rise when I fall.

- I will be a safe place for others.

- I will walk this path with open
  hands and an open heart

This is the embodiment of spiritual
awakening—not to escape the world, but
to *transform it* through your being.

**You, dear one, are the light the world
has been waiting for.**

Opening Meditation: Embodied Light

"Becoming the Light"

Sit in stillness and gently close your eyes. Bring your hands to your heart and take a deep, conscious breath.

Imagine a golden light rising from within you—soft, steady, and luminous. This is your soul's light— ancient, eternal, and true.

See it expanding outward from your heart... through your body... beyond your skin... illuminating the space around you.

Say softly or in your heart:
"I am the light. I embody the truth of who I am. I carry this light into the world with grace, courage, and love."

Rest in this radiant field. Let it hold you. Let it *be* you. When you are ready, begin this final chapter—fully present, fully alive.

Ways to Embody Your Light Daily

Practice	How to Do It
Mindful Movement	Walk barefoot in the grass. Stretch slowly. Dance Freely. Move with awareness.
Conscious Breath	Inhale: "I receive." Exhale: " shine. Use your breath to ground and expand your light.
Sacred Speech	Speak words that uplift, bless, and honor the truth. Silence can also be light.
Loving Action	Do one kind thing each day with full presence. Let your light ripple outward.
Energetic Boundaries	Protect your light by saying no to what dims your spirit. You are sacred space.

Ritual of Embodiment

The Mirror of Light Ritual

1. Light a candle and stand before a mirror.

2. Gaze gently into your own eyes. Say aloud:

"I see the light in you. I trust the path you walk. You are the one you've been waiting for."

3. Anoint your heart or third eye with oil or water.

4. Blow a kiss to your reflection. Thank yourself for showing up.

Final Reflection Prompts

- How has my light grown during this awakening journey?

- In what ways can I live more fully from the light of my soul?

- What legacy of love and healing do I want to leave in the world?

Final Blessing

"May your path be lit from within. May your presence   be healing. May your life be a living altar where Spirit walks beside you, always."

Tear-Out Pull-Out for Chapter 14: Embodying Your Light

Soul Guidance – "I Am Ready to Embody My Light"

You have journeyed through awakening, healing, release, and renewal. Now comes the sacred invitation: to embody your light. This means living your truth. Walking in love. Trusting your soul's wisdom. Letting your inner radiance guide your words, choices, and presence in the world. To embody your light is not about perfection—it's about alignment.
It's choosing peace even when it's hard. Speaking from your heart, even when your voice trembles. Holding space for both shadow and grace. It's being real, being present, being love.

Guidance for Living Your Divine Light:

- Trust your inner voice. You are more intuitive than you realize.

- Stay rooted in self-love. Even in doubt, even in growth—nourish yourself.

- Live from the inside out. Let your choices reflect your soul, not the outside noise.

- Surround yourself with light-bearers. Your energy is sacred—protect it.

- Shine in your way. Whether soft or bold, quiet or wild—your light is needed.

The world needs more souls who remember their light. Be that. Live that. Share that.

Light Activation Page – "My Soul's Light"

I am ready to embody my light by...

The ways I shine when I am fully me:

The ways I shine when I am fully me:

_____

_____

_____

_____

_____

_____

When I feel dim, I will remind myself...

_____

_____

_____

_____

_____

_____

Sacred Promise to Myself:

"I choose to walk in light. I honor my truth. I radiate love, courage, and purpose."

"I am the light. I am the way. I am whole."

Embodied Affirmations

Repeat these while looking in the mirror, walking in nature, or journaling:

- "I am the light in human form."
- "I radiate peace, joy, and compassion."
- "My presence is my prayer."
- "Every breath is a blessing."
- "I choose to live as love."

"I am the light. I am the way. I am whole."

Living As
Embodied Light

_____

_____

_____

_____

_____

_____

_____

_____

_____

_____

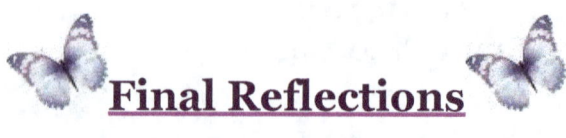

<u>Final Reflections</u>

_____

_____

_____

_____

_____

_____

_____

_____

_____

Tear-Out Moon Phase Reflection Pages

This section is your lunar companion—a space for reflection, ritual, and renewal.

Use these pages with each moon phase to set intentions, release what no longer serves you, celebrate your growth, and deepen your connection with the sacred rhythms of the Moon.

Let these pages be your journal, your altar, and your mirror.

MOON PHASES

For you to work with the moons energy we created a **two-page sprcad for each phase** of the Moon, beginning with:

New Moon –
Planting Seeds & Setting Intentions

Affirmation:
"I plant sacred intentions. I am open to new beginnings."

Guided Reflection Prompts:

- What do I want to invite into my life right now?

- What seeds am I ready to plant in my heart, work, or relationships?

- What is my soul calling me to begin?

Mini Ritual Space:

☐ Light a candle or write your intention in a sacred journal.

☐ Choose a symbol, crystal, or word to carry this new energy.

Notes

_____

_____

_____

_____

_____

_____

Waxing Moon – *Taking Aligned Action*

Affirmation:
"I move forward with clarity and courage."

Reflection Prompts:

- What small steps can I take toward my intention?
- Where am I being called to act in faith?
- What resources or support do I need
- right now?

Mini Ritual Space:

☐ Create a to-do list or vision board

☐ Work with herbs or oils that energize and inspire action.

Notes:

_____

_____

_____

_____

Full Moon –

Illumination & Celebration

Affirmation:

"I celebrate my growth. I shine in my truth."

Reflection Prompts:

- What has come to fullness in my life since the New Moon?
- What truth is being revealed to me now?
- How can I honor my efforts and celebrate my growth?

Mini Ritual Space:

☐ Dance, sing, or journal under the moonlight

☐ Cleanse your energy with moon-charged water or crystals

Notes:

_____

_____

_____

_____

Waning Moon –
Letting Go & Releasing

Affirmation:
"I release with love. I trust the flow of life."

Reflection Prompts:

- What am I ready to release or surrender?
- What emotional weight am I carrying that is no longer mine?
- How can I lovingly let go of what is no longer aligned?

Mini Ritual Space:

☐ Burn a release list safely

☐ Take a salt bath or smudge your space with herbs

Notes: (lined space)

Dark Moon – *Rest, Reflection & Inner Listening*

Affirmation:

"I rest in the unknown. I listen deeply to my soul."

Reflection Prompts:

- What wisdom is rising in the stillness?
- What dreams, signs, or inner nudges are guiding me?
- How can I offer myself grace and deep care right now.

Mini Ritual Space:

☐ Journal by candlelight

☐ Rest, nap, or meditate in silence

Notes:

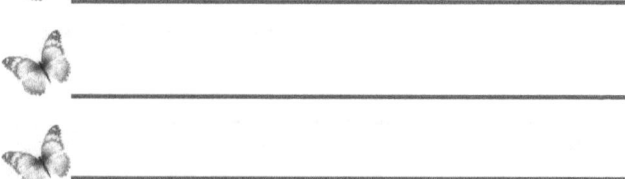

QUICK REFERENCE GUIDE - GLOSSARY

Section 1: Celestial Bodies & Cosmic Symbols

- **Sun** – Vitality, illumination, masculine energy *"Shine from within. Your light is meant to be seen."*
- **Moon** – Intuition, cycles, emotion *"Honor your rhythms. Everything has its season."*
- **Star** – Destiny, guidance, divine spark *"You are being led. Follow the light within and above."*
- **Planets** – Archetypes of growth and cosmic influence. *"The heavens move, and so do you. Your growth is cosmic."*
- **Moon Phases** – New, Waxing, Full, Waning, Dark. *"Your life follows the moon. Learn her language."*
- **Zodiac Signs** – Archetypal energies of the soul *"Each sign is a mirror—see yourself in the stars."*

Section 2: Energy & Chakra Symbols

1. Root Chakra – "I Am"

Meaning: The foundation of safety, survival, and grounding. It connects you to the Earth and your physical body.

2. Sacral Chakra – "I Feel"

Meaning: Center of emotions, creativity, pleasure, and relationships. It governs your ability to feel, enjoy, and create.

3. Solar Plexus Chakra – "I Do"

Meaning: The seat of personal power, will, and confidence. It fuels your actions, purpose, and self-worth.

4. Heart Chakra – "I Love"

Meaning: The bridge between body and spirit. It opens you to love, compassion, connection, and forgiveness.

5. Throat Chakra – "I Speak"

Meaning: The channel of communication and truth. It empowers you to express yourself clearly and honestly.

6. Third Eye Chakra – "I See"

Meaning: The center of inner vision, insight, and intuition. It helps you perceive beyond the visible world.

7. Crown Chakra – "I Know"

Meaning: Gateway to divine consciousness and unity. It connects you to higher wisdom, spirit, and oneness.

Section 3: Nature Elements & Tools

Core Elements

- **Salt** – Cleansing, grounding
  "Clear the old. Stand in your strength."
- **Fire** – Transformation, rebirth
  "Burn what no longer serves you."
- **Air** – Breath, spirit, clarity
  "Breathe in peace. Speak your truth."
- **Water** – Emotion, intuition, renewal
  "I release, I renew, I rise."
- **Earth** – Stability, nourishment, manifestation
  "I am rooted. I am whole."

Crystals & Their Sacred Energy

- **Clear Quartz** – Amplification, clarity, spiritual light.
- **Amethyst** – Protection, intuition, peace.
- **Rose Quartz** – Love, emotional healing, compassion.
- **Citrine** – Joy, abundance, confidence.
- **Black Tourmaline** – Grounding, protection, energy clearing.

Herbs for Ritual & Healing

- **Sage** – Purification, energy clearing.
- **Lavender** – Calm, sacred blessing, restful energy.
- **Rosemary** – Clarity, memory, psychic protection.
- **Palo Santo** – Spiritual connection, positivity.
- **Mugwort** – Dreamwork, intuition, psychic opening.

Section 4:
Ritual Objects & Tools

- **Anointing Oils** – Blessings for the body, chakras, and sacred tools
  "I anoint my body as a vessel of light."
- **Bell** – Clears stagnant energy, calls in spirit or intention
  "Let this sound awaken the sacred within me."
- **Candle-** Lights the way home
  "With flame, I focus and invite the divine."
- **Cauldron** – Symbol of transformation, used for fire rituals, burning herbs, or water blessings
  "From the ashes, I rise anew."
- **Chalice** – Sacred feminine vessel, used for offering water, wine, or moon elixirs
  "I open to receive divine nourishment."
- **Crystal Grid** – An intentional layout of stones to amplify energy or manifestation
  "I weave sacred energy into the web of becoming."
- **Feather** – Carries prayers to the heavens, represents air and divine messages
  "With each breath, I remember I am free."

- **Offering Bowl** – For holding intentions, herbs, crystals, or symbolic gifts to Spirit.
  "I offer with gratitude and reverence."
- **Pendulum** – Used for divination, receiving intuitive guidance
  "I trust the wisdom that moves through me."
- **Sacred Cord / Ribbon** – Used in tying rituals, cord cutting, or symbolic unity.
  "I bind or release with love and purpose."
- **Shell** – Used to hold herbs for burning or to represent water; linked to the ocean and intuition.
  "May the wisdom of the sea guide me inward."
- **Smudge Stick**
  "Clear the air, clear your spirit."
- **Sound Tools** – Tuning forks, singing bowls, drums or rattles used for vibration and energy shifts
  "Let the rhythm awaken the soul."
- **Wand** – Directs energy, focuses intention, connects above and below.
  "I send my energy with clarity and grace."

Section 5: Spirit Animals

- **Bat** – Rebirth, transition, intuition
- **Bear** – Strength, grounding, inner wisdom
- **Bison** – Abundance, sacred connection, resilience
- **Butterfly** – Transformation, joy, soul growth
- **Cat** – Independence, curiosity, mystery
- **Coyote** – Trickster, adaptability, sacred humor
- **Crow** – Magic, truth, shape-shifting
- **Deer** – Gentleness, grace, sensitivity
- **Dog** – Loyalty, protection, unconditional love
- **Dolphin** – Playfulness, communication, harmony
- **Dragonfly** – Illusion, lightness, transformation
- **Eagle** – Divine sight, spiritual power, higher vision
- **Elephant** – Wisdom, memory, gentle leadership
- **Fox** – Cleverness, agility, camouflage
- **Frog** – Cleansing, renewal, emotional release
- **Hawk** – Clarity, messages, perspective
- **Horse** – Freedom, drive, spiritual journey
- **Hummingbird** – Joy, sweetness, presence
- **Lion** – Courage, leadership, heart strength
- **Monkey** – Playfulness, intelligence, trickster energy
- **Owl** – Intuition, mystery, seeing the unseen
- **Peacock** – Beauty, truth, resurrection
- **Phoenix** – Death & rebirth, eternal soul, transformation

- **Rabbit** – Fertility, gentleness, abundance
- **Raccoon** – Resourcefulness, disguise, curiosity
- **Snake** – Transformation, healing, kundalini energy
- **Spider** – Creativity, destiny weaving, feminine power
- **Tiger** – Power, sensuality, wildness
- **Turtle** – Longevity, protection, grounded wisdom
- **Wolf** – Guidance, loyalty, freedom

Section 6: Sacred Symbols

Anchor –Stability, hope, grounding amidst change
- **Ankh** – Eternal life, sacred union, divine feminine
- **Arrow** – Direction, movement, purpose
- **Chalice** – Receptivity, sacred vessel, divine feminine
- **Crescent Moon** – New beginnings, feminine energy
- **Eye of Horus** – Protection, healing, divine sight
- **Feather** – Lightness, prayer, spiritual communication
- **Hamsa Hand** – Divine protection, blessing, warding evil
- **Heart** – Love, emotional truth, soul connection

- **Infinity** – Limitless potential, eternity
- **Keys** – Unlocking mysteries, spiritual authority
- **Labyrinth** – Inner journey, meditation, soul alignment
- **Lotus** – Spiritual awakening, purity, enlightenment
- **Mandala** – Harmony, spiritual focus, sacred geometry
- **Om** – Universal sound, divine vibration, unity
- **Pentacle** – Protection, earth wisdom, elemental balance
- **Rainbow** – Divine promise, unity, higher realms
- **Sacred Circle** – Wholeness, protection, the infinite
- **Spiral** – Soul journey, evolution, spiritual expansion
- **Star (5-pointed)** – Light, divine connection, guidance
- **Tree of Life** – Connection, rooted wisdom, oneness
- **Triskelion** – Personal growth, action, life cycles
- **Triple Moon** – Divine feminine, life rhythms, intuition
- **Wings** – Freedom, angelic presence, higher perspective
- **Yin Yang** – Balance, duality, cosmic harmony

Special Request from the Author

Dear Spirit Sister or Brother,

If you have enjoyed or were enlightened by this guided workbook. Please join me before you put it away, to bless and guide this wonderful offering forward to others on their journey towards self-discovery and enlightenment.

Please take this prayer, affirmation, meditation and my gratitude with you into your meditation to send it forward with

Love & Light.

Blessed Be

Affirmation of Sacred Circulation
"This workbook is a sacred gift."

It flows effortlessly into the lives of those who need it most. It awakens, heals, and inspires. Its light cannot be hidden—it shines through me into the world."
Repeat aloud or write into your altar journal.
Speak it under the light of the moon, or whenever you feel called to ignite its journey.

Meditation for Divine Distribution

Use this meditation to energetically align with the soul mission of your workbook.

1. **Sit comfortably** with the workbook in your hands or placed on your altar.
2. **Breathe deeply**, envisioning a radiant golden light forming at your heart center.
3. With each inhale, imagine the light expanding. With each exhale, send that light into the workbook.
4. Now see this golden light forming a butterfly—our sacred symbol—taking flight.
5. Visualize dozens... then hundreds... then thousands of butterflies, each one gently landing in someone's hands, home, or heart.

Whisper: *"Go where you are needed. Find those who are ready. Be a guide, a light, a friend."* Sit in stillness for a few more breaths, holding this vision.

When complete, place your hands over the workbook and say: **"I release this offering in divine trust. May it fulfill its sacred purpose."**

Denise Jensen

Denise Jensen is a spiritual teacher, intuitive guide, and founder of the Lighten Up Spiritualality LLC. Known as "Spirit Sister" to those she walks beside, she has dedicated her life to creating sacred spaces for healing, awakening, and joyful connection.

With decades of experience in energy work, astrology, ritual, and spiritual mentorship, Denise brings a warm, grounded presence to every soul she touches.

Through her workbook Awakening and her community offerings, Denise helps others trust their inner voice, reclaim their light, and walk the path of the heart. She believes that spirituality is not about becoming someone new—it's about remembering who you truly are.

Facebook: Lightenupspirituality
www.lightenupspirituality.com
or email

Lightenup02@yahoo.com